The Great Freedom Fighters of India

By

Mr. JUBER HAWALDAR
M.Sc., B.Ed.

Department of Physics
*Sri. Channabasaveshwar Post Graduate Study
& Research Center Bhalki - 585328*

This Book is dedicated to all the Freedom Fighters of India. Who Sacrifieses their lives for our freedom.

CONTENT

FREEDOM FIGHTERS OF INDIA & THEIR SLOGANS

Freedom Fighters	Their Slogans
Netaji Subhash Chandra Bose	'Jai Hind' 'Tum Mujhe Khoon Do, Main Tumhe Aazadi Doonga'
Maulana Hasrat Mohani	Inquilab Zindabad
Mohandas Karamchand Gandhi	'Do or Die' "Agrezo Bharat Chhodo"
Yusuf Meherally	'Quit India'
Bankim Chandra Chatterji	'Vande Mataram'
Muhammad Iqbal	"Sare Jahan Se Accha Hindustan Hamara"
Pandit Madan Mohan Malviya	"Satyameva Jayate"
Bal Gangadhar Tilak	"Swaraj mera janam sidh adhikar hai, aur mai ise lekar rahunga"
Chandrashekar Azad	"Ab bhi jiska khoon khaula nahi wo pani hai, jo desh ke kaam na aaye who bekar jawani hai"
Jawaharlal Nehru	"Aaram haram hai"
Lala Lajpat Rai	"Simon Go Back"
Lal Bahadur Shastri	Jai Jawan Jai Kishan

1. Sardar Vallabhbhai Patel

Vallabhbhai Jhaverbhai Patel, commonly known as Sardar Vallabhai Patel, was an Indian independence nationalist and barrister who served as the first Deputy Prime Minister and Home Minister of India from 1947 to 1950.

Born: 31 October 1875, Nadiad

Died: 15 December 1950, Mumbai

Spouse: Jhaverba Patel (m. 1893–1909)

Children: Dahyabhai Patel, Maniben Patel

Awards: Bharat Ratna

Party: Indian National Congress

'The '*Iron man of India*' Sardar Vallabhbhai Patel is one of the most vital pathfinder in the Indian history of Independence. Known for his patriotism for the country, Patel's primary motivation was to expel the British out of the country. He was one of the prominent Indian barristers, politicians and leading figures of the country. As the founding father of the "Republic of India" he played a pivotal role in integrating the provinces and making the Nation united. To recognize his monumental contribution and service to the Nation, 31st October, birthday of Sardar Vallabh Bhai Patel is celebrated as the National Unity Day

2. Pandit Jawaharlal Nehru

Jawaharlal Nehru was an Indian anti-colonial nationalist, secular humanist, social democrat, and author who was a central figure in India during the middle of the 20th century. Nehru was a principal leader of the Indian nationalist movement in the 1930s and 1940s.

Born: 14 November 1889, Prayagraj

Died: 27 May 1964, New Delhi

Spouse: Kamala Nehru (m. 1916–1936)

Previous offices: Minister of Defence of India (1962–1962)

Children: Indira Gandhi

Parents: Motilal Nehru, Swarup Rani Nehru

'The Architect of Modern India' - Pandit Jawaharlal Nehru was India's first and longest serving Prime Minister also known as a visionary and an influential leader in the Indian independence movement. Pt. Nehru spent years in jail to win freedom. The book 'The Discovery of India' was written by him while he was in jail. As a firm believer in Nation building, his first commitment was to make India a self-sufficient economy. Pt. Nehru is popularly known for setting up the strong foundation in industrial powerhouse, military power, space and established network of educational institutions like IITs and IIMs. Being a favorite amongst the children as 'Chacha Nehru', his birthday -14th November is celebrated as Children's Day in India.

3. Mahatma Gandhi

Mohandas Karamchand Gandhi was an Indian lawyer, anti-colonial nationalist and political ethicist who employed nonviolent resistance to lead the successful campaign for India's independence from British rule. He inspired movements for civil rights and freedom across the world.

Born: 2 October 1869, Porbandar

Grandchildren: Gopalkrishna Gandhi, Arun Manilal Gandhi

Great grandchildren: Leela Gandhi, Tushar Gandhi, Kirti Menon

Assassinated: 30 January 1948, Birla House, New Delhi

Parents: Karamchand Gandhi, Putlibai Gandhi

Spouse: Kasturba Gandhi (m. 1883–1944)

Children: Harilal Gandhi, Ramdas Gandhi, Devdas Gandhi, Manilal Gandhi

'Father of the Nation' - Mahatma Gandhi was a great leader and a social reformer, a role model for the entire nation and abroad. With his supreme sacrifice and noble ideals of Satya (truth) and Ahimsa (nonviolence), Mahatma Gandhi contributed tirelessly and selflessly in India's struggle for Independence. He touched life of every Indian through his ideal thought of unity and social upliftment, and use of Swadeshi goods. He believed in simple living and high thinking. He was the champion of democracy and highly opposed to dictatorial rule. His birthday on 2nd October is celebrated across the entire world as the International Day of Non-violence.

4. Subhash Chandra Bose

Subhas Chandra Bose was an Indian nationalist whose defiance of British authority in India made him a hero among many Indians, but his wartime alliances with Nazi Germany and Imperial Japan left a legacy vexed by authoritarianism, anti-Semitism, and military failure.

Born: 23 January 1897, Cuttack

Organizations founded: Azad Hind, All India Forward Bloc

Children: Anita Bose Pfaff

Parents: Janakinath Bose, Prabhabati Bose

Movies: Netaji Bose & The Lost Treasure, Pandit Nehru

Height: 1.74 m

Netaji Subhash Chandra Bose, was a great freedom fighter and a patriot. He was a fearless leader who left no stone unturned in his quest to attain freedom, he founded the Azad Hind Army or the Indian National Army. For his revolutionary movements, Bose had been to jail several times. Several Indian residents and Indian prisoners of war participated in his free Indian army to fight against the British rule bravely. Subhash Chandra Bose inspired his soldiers with his great words of "Give me blood, I will give you freedom" to liberate motherland from the British rule. Subhas Chandra Bose's birth anniversary on January 23 is celebrated as Parakram Diwas . Subhas Chandra Bose was an Indian revolutionary prominent in the independence movement against British rule of India. Bose died from third-degree burns after his plane crashed in Japanese Taiwan on 18 August 1945. Some Indians did not believe that the crash had occurred, expecting Bose to return to secure India's independence.

5. Shaheed Bhagat Singh

Bhagat Singh was an Indian anti-colonial revolutionary, who participated in the mistaken murder of a junior British police officer in December 1928 in what was to be retaliation for the death of an Indian nationalist.

Born: 28 September 1907, Banga, Pakistan

Died: 23 March 1931 (age 23 years), Lahore Central Jail, Lahore, Pakistan

Siblings: Bibi Parkash Kaur, Kultar Singh, Bibi Amar Kaur, Kulbir Singh, Bibi Shakuntla, Rajinder Singh, Jagat Singh, Ranbir Singh

Organization founded: Naujawan Bharat Sabha

Parents: Sardar Kishan Singh Sandhu, Vidyavati

Height: 1.83 m

Bhagat Singh was a hero of the early 20th-century Indian independence movement. He was a vocal critic of British rule in India and was involved in two high-profile attacks on British authorities—one on a local police chief and the other on the Central Legislative Assembly in Delhi. Shaheed Bhagat Singh was one of the most influential revolutionaries of the Indian Independence Movement. He believes that the only way to drive the British out of the country would be through armed rebellion. Jallianwala tragedy in the year 1912 left a very deep scar in his heart, at the age of 12 years. He brought a revolution in the national movement against the British Rule. He was the active supporter of the Swadeshi Movement. Bhagat Singh was only 23 years old when he sacrificed himself for the country and it became an inspiration for the youth. His death proved to be a motivation for many Indians to join the struggle of independence. Revolutionary freedom fighters Bhagat Singh, Shivaram Rajguru and Sukhdev Thapar were hanged to death by the British government for their activities on March 23, 1931, at the Lahore Jail. This day is observed as 'Martyrs' Day' in India.

6. Bal Gangadhar Tilak

Bal Gangadhar Tilak, endeared as Lokmanya, was an Indian nationalist, teacher, and an independence activist. He was one third of the Lal Bal Pal triumvirate. The British colonial authorities called him "The father of the Indian unrest".

Born: 23 July 1856, Ratnagiri

Died: 1 August 1920 (age 64 years), Mumbai

Organizations founded: Fergusson College, Deccan Education Society, New English School, Pune

Spouse: Satyabhamabai Tilak (m. 1871–1920)

Education: Government Law College, Mumbai (1878–1879)

Children: Sridhar Balwant Tilak, Vishwanath Balwant Tilak, Rambhau Balwant Tilak

The father of the Indian revolution'- Bal Gangadhar Tilak was a Nationalist Indian leader and a freedom fighter. Bal Gangadhar Tilak was the first Indian leader to give the slogan, *"Freedom is my birth right and I shall have it"*. For his anti-imperialistic activities, he was sent to jail many times. During his imprisonment, he wrote his famous commentary on Srimadbhagwat Gita- Gita Rahasaya. Shri Tilak was in fact, a profound scholar of Indian history and culture and also wrote a book on Vedas Arctic Home in the Vedas. He vehemently opposed the Partition of Bengal (1905) under the Viceroyalty of Lord Curzon. Lifelong, he strived for nationalism. His speeches and writings reflect his profound social and political ideas which are of immense value to mankind. Bal Gangadhar Tilak was a scholar, mathematician, philosopher, and ardent nationalist who helped lay the foundation for India's independence by building his own defiance of British rule into a national movement.

7. Lal Bahadur Shastri

Lal Bahadur Shastri was an Indian politician and statesman who served as the prime minister of India from 1964 to 1966. He previously served as the sixth home minister of India from 1961 to 1963. Shastri was born to Sharad Prasad Srivastava and Ramdulari Devi in Mughalsarai on 2 October 1904.

Born: 2 October 1904, Mughalsarai

Died: 11 January 1966 (age 61 years), Tashkent, Uzbekistan

Previous offices: Prime Minister of India (1964–1966)

Children: Anil Shastri, Sunil Shastri, Kusum Shastri, Suman Shastri, Hari Krishna Shastri, Ashok Shastri

Spouse: Lalita Shastri (m. 1928–1966)

Education: Mahatma Gandhi Kashi Vidyapith University (1925)

Parents: Sharada Prasad Srivastava, Ramdulari Devi

Man of Peace- Lal Bahadur Shastri - A thoughtful leader, a visionary and a freedom fighter. Shastri Ji heralded great reformation in the country through several path breaking initiatives. He was the second Prime Minister of India. He gave a famous slogan "JaiJawan Jai Kisan". Lal Bahadur Shastri tackled many elementary problems like food shortage, unemployment, and poverty. To overcome the acute food shortage, Shastri ji asked the experts to devise a long-term strategy. This was the beginning of the famous "Green Revolution". "Bharat Ratna" Shastri ji will always be counted as one of the greatest martyrs and leaders of the country.

8. Lala Lajpat Rai

Lala Lajpat Rai (28 January 1865 - 17 November 1928) was an Indian Punjabi author and politician who is chiefly remembered as a leader in the Indian Independence movement. He was popularly known as Punjab Kesari. He was one third of the Lal Bal Pal triumvirate.

Born: 28 January 1865, Dhudike

Died: 17 November 1928 (age 63 years), Lahore, Pakistan

Organizations founded: Hindu Mahasabha, All India Trade Union Congress, Servants of the People Society

Children: Pyarelal Agrawal, Amrit Rai Agrawal, Parvati Agrawal

Parents: Gulab Devi, Radha Krishan

Party: Indian National Congress

'Lion of Punjab' Lala Lajpat Rai, popularly known as "Punjab Kesari", was an Indian independence activist, author, politician, freedom struggler who played a pivotal role in the Indian Independence movement. `Lala Lajpat Rai was the founder of several organizations in the late 19th and early 20th centuries. He was the driving force behind the establishment of Punjab National Bank. Inspired by Swami Dayanand Saraswati's Hindu reformist movement, he was known for his fiery speeches and inspire people to participate in the freedom movement. In 1928 he introduced the legislative assembly resolution for a boycott of the British Simon Commission on constitutional reform. Rai was attacked by police officers during a peaceful demonstration against the commission in Lahore on October 30, 1928. He succumbed to his injuries on November 17.

9. Pandit Madan Mohan Malaviya

Madan Mohan Malaviya; born Madan Mohan Srivastava was an Indian scholar, educational reformer and politician notable for his role in the Indian independence movement. He was president of the Indian National Congress three times and the founder of Akhil Bharat Hindu Mahasabha.

Born: 25 December 1861, Prayagraj

Died: 12 November 1946 (age 84 years), Varanasi

Organizations founded: Banaras Hindu University

Education: University of Allahabad, University of Calcutta

Party: Hindu Mahasabha

Awards: Bharat Ratna

Mahamana - Pandit Madan Mohan Malaviya, was an Indian scholar, educational reformer and politician made an immense contribution to the Indian independence movement. He was the founder of the Banaras Hindu University (BHU), He also founded a highly influential, English-newspaper "The Leader". Pt. Malaviya was given a title 'Mahamana' by Nobel laureate Rabindranath Tagore. He was posthumously conferred with Bharat Ratna, on December 24, 2014. The slogan "Satyameva Jayate" is also a legacy given to the nation by Pandit Malaviya. Bharat Dharma Mahamandala was founded by Pandit Madan Mohan Malaviya and Pandit Din Dayal Sharma in Varanasi in 1887 AD. He established Hindu Mahasabha in 1915. Malviya decided to establish a university in Varanasi. He got as donation the land required to establish the university from the then King of Varanasi. He travelled across the whole nation and collected approximately 64 lac rupees. That is why he is known as the Teacher of the Nation.

10. Chandra Shekhar Azad

Chandra Shekhar Sitaram Tiwari, popularly known as Chandra Shekhar Azad, was an Indian revolutionary who reorganised the Hindustan Republican Association under its new name of Hindustan Socialist.

Born: 23 July 1906, Bhavra

Died: 27 February 1931 (age 24 years), Chandrashekhar Azad Park, Prayagraj

Parents: Jagrani Devi, Sitaram Tiwari

Siblings: Sukhdev

Full name: Chandra Shekhar Tiwari

Movement: Indian Independence Movement

Organization: Hindustan Socialist Republican Association

Chandrashekhar Azad was a great Indian freedom fighter. His fierce patriotism and courage inspired many people to enter freedom struggle. He also led the chief strategist of the Hindustan Socialist Republican Association (HSRA). Chandrashekhar Azad was on the hit list of British Police. British Police badly wanted to capture him dead or alive. British Police captured Shri Azad in severely injured condition. He used his last bullet to kill himself but did not surrenderto the British Police. Thelegacy of Chandra Shekhar Azad will be remembered for his unconditional love and selfless sacrifice for the country. Known for his organizational skills, Azad played a key role in reorganizing the HRA as the Hindustan Socialist Republican Association after most of the HRA's members had been killed or imprisoned. His crimes had made him a wanted man, but Azad was able to elude the police and its informants for several years.

11. Ram Prasad Bismil

Ram Prasad Bismil was an Indian poet, writer, and revolutionary who fought against British Raj, participating in the Mainpuri Conspiracy of 1918, and the Kakori Conspiracy of 1925. He composed in Urdu and Hindi under pen names Ram, Agyat and Bismil, becoming widely known under the latter. He was also a translator.

Born: 11 June 1897, Shahjahanpur

Died: 19 December 1927 (age 30 years), Gorakhpur Jail, Gorakhpur

Parents: Moolmati, Murlidhar

Nationality: British, British Raj, Indian

Criminal charges: Robbery

Organization: Hindustan Republican Association

Today, he is one of India's most revered freedom fighters, known as much for his revolutionary zeal as for his poetic profundity.

The slogan of Ram Prasad Bismil is
"Sarfaroshi ki tamanna ab hamare dil mein hai, dekhna ki zor kitna baazu-e-qatil mein hai." (The desire for revolution is in our hearts, we shall see how much strength lies in the arms of the enemy.)

Sarfaroshi Ki Tamanna is an Urdu patriotic poem written by Bismil Azimabadi as a dedication to young freedom fighters of the Indian independence movement. This poem was popularized by Ram Prasad Bismil.

The quote by Ram Prasad Bismil is
History is the proof, I will reborn again, and will serve the nation. I will abolish the name of slavery from the society, and i will bring freedom there.

12. Rani Laxmi Bai
(Lakshmibai Newalkar)

Lakshmibai dressed as a sowar

Queen consort of Jhansi

Tenure : 1843 – 21 November 1853

Regent of Jhansi : (pretendence)

Regency : 21 November 1853 – 1858

Monarch : Damodar Rao (disputed)

Successor : Position abolished

Born : Manikarnika Tambe

19 November 1828

Benares, Kingdom of Kashi-Benares

Died : 18 June 1858 (aged 29)

Gwalior, Gwalior State, Company India

Spouse : Gangadhar Rao Newalkar

(m. 1842; died 1853)

Issue : Damodar Rao

      Anand Rao (adopted)

Dynasty : Newalkar (by marriage)

Father : Moropant Tambe

Mother : Bhagirathi Sapre

Rani Laxmibai also called the Rani of Jhansi was a pivotal figure in the Indian Revolt of 1857. She is also regarded as one of the greatest freedom fighters in India. Rani Lakshmibai was born on 19 November 1828 in the town of Varanasi. She was named Manikarnika Tambe and was nicknamed Manu. Lakshmi Bai is remembered for her valour during the Indian Mutiny of 1857–58. During a siege of the fort of Jhansi, Bai offered stiff resistance to the invading forces and did not surrender even after her troops were overwhelmed. She was later killed in combat after having successfully assaulted Gwalior. She was one of the first women freedom fighters of India who revolted against the British in 1857.

13. Mangal Pandey

Mangal Pandey was an Indian soldier who played a key role in the events taking place just before the outbreak of the Indian rebellion of 1857. He was a sepoy in the 34th Bengal Native Infantry regiment of the British East India Company. In 1984, the Indian government issued a postage stamp to remember him.

Born: 19 July 1827, Nagwa

Died: 8 April 1857 (age 29 years), Barrackpur Cantonment

Parents: Divakar Pandey, Abhairani Pandey

Allegiance: East India Company

Known for: Indian independence fighter

Rank: Sepoy

Service/branch: Bengal Army

Mangal Pandey was born on 31 December 1972 to a family of farmers in Bhirgu Baliya, Maharajgunj, Siwan district, Bihar. He was the elder of two born to Awadhesh Pandey and Premlata Pandey. He married Urmila Pandey on 19 April 1998. She is from Bhitti "Sahabuddin", "Baniyapur", Saran District.

Mangal Pandey's actions in 1857 sparked the Indian Mutiny, also often called India's First War of Independence. The rebellion led to the abolition of the British East India Company in favour of direct British rule. This initiated a period when heightened Indian nationalism steered India toward independence. Indian freedom fighter, Mangal Pandey, killed two British officials - Hugeson and Baugh on March 29, 1857, in Calcutta. Mangal Pandey was one of the prominent faces of the revolt of 1857 who was given death sentence by the British in a fear that he would have been responsible for the massive outrage during the revolt. In 1857, Barrackpore was the scene of an incident that some credit with starting of the Indian Rebellion of 1857: an Indian soldier, Mangal Pandey, attacked his British commander, and was subsequently court-martialled.

14. Nana Sahib

Nana Saheb Peshwa II, born as Dhondu Pant, was an Indian aristocrat and fighter, who led the rebellion in Cawnpore during the 1857 rebellion against the East India Company.

Born: 19 May 1824, Bithoor

Died: 24 September 1859 (age 35 years), Nepal

Parents: Baji Rao II, Narayan Bhatt, Ganga Bai

Children: Baya Bai

Full name: Dhondu Pant,

Great-grandparents: Baji Rao I, Kashibai

Grandparents: Raghunath Rao, Anandibai

Nana Sahib (born 1824 as Dhondu Pant) was the adopted son of the Maratha Peshwa Baji Rao II whose kingdom had been annexed by the British following the 3rd Maratha War. He was brought up in exile in Bithur. Nana Sahib was a prominent leader in the Indian Mutiny of 1857–58. Although he did not plan the outbreak, he assumed leadership of the sepoys (British-employed Indian soldiers). During the 1857 uprising in Cawnpore (Kanpur), he led the "sepoys" (British-employed Indian soldiers) and successfully forced the British entrenchment to surrender. Nana eventually took control of the city. A later massacre at the Satichaura Ghat, however, flipped the tables. Nana himself was reported to be living in the interior of Nepal. Some early government records maintained that he died in Nepal after a tiger attacked him during a hunt on 24 September 1859 but other record differs on the matter. Nana's ultimate fate was never known. This humiliated him and made him to take part in the Revolt of 1857. A famous slogan of him is as follows: "A famous person to themselves, they don't get up in the morning and think, I'm famous. I'm not famous to me.

15. Annie Besant

Born :   **Annie Wood**
1 October 1847
Clapham, London, United Kingdom
of Great Britain and Ireland

Died :   **20 September 1933 (aged 85)**
Adyar, Chinglepet District, Madras
Presidency, British India
(now Chennai, Tamil Nadu, India)

Known for :   **Theosophist, women's rights activist, writer and orator**

Political party :   **Indian National Congress**
Social Democratic Federation

Movement :   **Indian independence movement**

Spouse :   **Frank Besant**
(m. 1867; div. 1873)

Children :   Arthur, Mabel, Jiddu Krishnamurti
              (adopted)

Annie Besant was a brave and outspoken woman. She was a freedom fighter, educationalist, feminist, and activist. She remained a Theosophical Society member until she died at the age of 85. She is well-known for establishing the Indian Home Rule League in India along the lines of the Irish Home League. Besant first visited India in 1893 and later settled there, becoming involved in the Indian nationalist movement. In 1916 she established the Indian Home Rule League, of which she became president. She was also a leading member of the Indian National Congress.

<u>Reforms did Annie Besant</u>

Educational Reforms:
1) Annie Besant advocated for research into ancient Indian religions, philosophies, and doctrines.
2) She also founded the Central Hindu School in 1898 at varanasi, to promote education.
3) Later it has became the Banaras Hindu University with the efforts of Madan Mohan Malaviya in 1916.

16. Dr. Rajendra Prasad

Rajendra Prasad was an Indian politician, lawyer, journalist and scholar who served as the first president of India from 1950 to 1962. He joined the Indian National Congress during the Indian independence movement and became a major leader from the region of Bihar.

Born: 3 December 1884, Ziradei

Died: 28 February 1963 (age 78 years), Patna

Previous offices: President of India (1950–1962)

Parents: Mahadev Sahai, Kamleshwari Devi

Spouse: Rajvanshi Devi (m. 1896–1962)

Education: Department of Law, University of Calcutta (1915)

Presidential term: 26 January 1950 – 13 May 1962

Dr. Rajendra Prasad served as the first President of India, holding the office from January 26, 1950, until May 13, 1962. As president, Prasad established a tradition for non-partisanship and independence for the office-bearer and retired from Congress party politics. Although a ceremonial head of state, Prasad encouraged the development of education in India and advised government on several occasions. As the President of the Constituent Assembly and subsequently as the President of India for two consecutive terms, Dr. Rajendra Prasad played a very important role in shaping the destiny of the nation and left an indelible imprint of his personality on our national life and polity. In 1946, Rajendra Prasad joined the Interim Government of India as the Minister of Food and Agriculture. As a firm believer in the maximization of agricultural production, he crafted the slogan "Grow More Food." Rajendra Prasad was one of the foremost disciples of Gandhi ji and he played a crucial role in Indian freedom struggle. His role was instrumental during Non-Cooperation Movement, Salt Satyagrah and Quit India Movement alongside other freedom fighters.

17. Aruna Asaf Ali

Aruna Asaf Ali was an Indian educator, political activist, and publisher. An active participant in the Indian independence movement, she is widely remembered for hoisting the Indian National flag at the Gowalia Tank maidan, Bombay during the Quit India Movement in 1942.

Born: 16 July 1909, Kalka

Died: 29 July 1996 (age 87 years), New Delhi

Spouse: Asaf Ali (m. 1928–1953)

Awards: Bharat Ratna, Lenin Peace Prize, Jawaharlal Nehru Award for International Understanding, Padma Vibhushan

Parents: Upendranath Ganguly, Ambalika Devi

Education: All Saints' College Nainital, Convent Of Sacred Heart Lahore

Personal life. In 1928, he married Aruna Asaf Ali, a marriage that raised eyebrows on the grounds of religion (Asaf Ali was a Muslim while Aruna was a Hindu) and age difference (Aruna was 20 years junior to him). It was her chivalrous behaviour that gave her the title of 'Heroine of 1942' movement or 'Grand Old Lady' of Independence Movement. She began the Quit India Movement by hoisting the Indian Flag at the Gowalia Tank ground. Also known as the Grand Old Lady of the Indian Freedom Struggle, Aruna Asaf Ali hoisted the tricolour Indian flag at the Gowalia Tank Maidan in 1942. Aruna Asaf Ali took part in many non-violent agitations during the Salt Satyagraha. For this, she was promptly arrested by the colonial authorities. Upon release, she was not politically active but at the end of 1942, she became an active member of the underground movement.

18. Ashfaqulla Khan

Ashfaqulla Khan was freedom fighter in the Indian independence movement against British rule and co-founder of the Hindustan Republican Association, later to become the Hindustan Socialist Republican Association.

Born: 22 October 1900, Shahjahanpur

Died: 19 December 1927 (age 27 years), Faizabad

Parents: Shafiq Ullah Khan, Mazhoor-Un-Nisa

Siblings: Riyasat Ullah Khan

Known for: Being a mastermind behind the Kakori train robbery

Movement: Indian independence

Organization: Hindustan Republican Association

Ashfaqulla Khan was born in 1900 at Shahjahanpur, Uttar Pradesh and was a freedom fighter who actively fought against the British forces. After the 'Chauri Chaura' incident in 1922 when Mahatma Gandhi decided to withdraw the movement, Ashfaqulla was dissatisfied. The case for the Kakori dacoity was concluded by imposing the death sentence on Bismil, Khan, Lahiri, and Roshan. The others were given life sentences. Khan was sentenced to death by hanging and executed on 19 December 1927 at the Faizabad Jail. Ashfaqullah closed the Holy Quran that he was reading, put it under his arm, stood up and said, "Let's go". He took two steps at a time to the gallows. Before being hanged, he tied the Quran on his chest and recited the 'Kalma'. Ramprasad Bismil and Ashfaqulla Khan 'Warsi' shared an especially close bond. They were both Urdu poets: Bismil's poem Sarfaroshi ki tamanna (Aspiration for sacrifice) was a virtual anthem for the HSRA revolutionaries. Ashfaq was inspired by Bismil's example to join the revolutionary movement.

19. Vinayak Damodar Savarkar

Vinayak Damodar Savarkar was an Indian politician, activist and writer. Savarkar developed the Hindu nationalist political ideology of Hindutva while confined at Ratnagiri in 1922. He was a leading figure in the Hindu Mahasabha. The prefix "Veer" has been applied to his name by his followers.

Born: 28 May 1883, Bhagur

Died: 26 February 1966 (age 82 years), Mumbai

Children: Vishwas Savarkar, Prabhakar Savarkar, Prabhat Chiplunkar

Spouse: Yamunabai Savarkar (m. 1901–1963)

Party: Hindu Mahasabha

Organizations founded: Abhinav Bharat Society, Free India Society

The colonial authorities provided a bungalow for him and he was allowed visitors. During his internment, he met influential people such as Mahatma Gandhi and B. R. Ambedkar. Nathuram Godse, who later assassinated Gandhi, also met Savarkar for the first time as a nineteen-year-old in 1929. Shri Ganesh Vaishampayan gave the title of Veer to Veer Savarkar in 1923 in a poem. As per earliest available records he was given title of Swatantraveer in 1924 by author Sadashiv Rajaram Ranade in a short biography called Swatantraveer Savarkar Yanche Sankshipt Charitra. Arrested in 1910 for his connections with the revolutionary group India House. One of the charges on Savarkar was abetment to murder of Nashik Collector Jackson and the second was waging a conspiracy under Indian Penal Code 121-A against the King emperor. Hindus, according to Savarkar, are those who consider India to be the land in which their ancestors lived, as well as the land in which their religion originated: "one for whom India is both Fatherland and Holyland".

20. Begum Hazrat Mahal

Begum Hazrat Mahal, also known as the Begum of Awadh, was the second wife of Nawab of Awadh Wajid Ali Shah, and the regent of Awadh in 1857–1858. She is known for the leading role she had in the rebellion against the British East India Company during the Indian Rebellion of 1857.

Born: Faizabad

Died: 7 April 1879, Kathmandu, Nepal

Spouse: Wajid Ali Shah (m. ?–1879)

Children: Birjis Qadr

Begum Hazrat Mahal was one of the most important women leaders during the First War of Independence, who operated from Lucknow in Uttar Pradesh. After the recapture of Lucknow by the British in March 1858, she was compelled to escape towards Nepal along with other leaders of the revolutionary movement. During the Indian Rebellion of 1857, Begum Hazrat Mahal's band of supporters rebelled against the forces of the British under the leadership of Raja Jailal Singh; they seized control of Lucknow, and she took power as the guardian of her minor son, Prince Birjis Qadr, whom she had declared as the ruler (Wali) of Awadh. Begum Hazrat Mahal. As a child, she was sold by her parents due to their poverty to royal agents. Soon she became a courtesan by profession as she entered the royal harem as a Khawasin where she was promoted to a Pari and was known as Mahek Pari. Begum Hazrat Mahal's band of supporters, led by Raja Jalal Singh rebelled against the forces of the British. After the recapture of Lucknow by rebel forces led by the Begum and her allies, she crowned her 11-year-old son Birjis Qadras the ruler of Avadh. She died for the great cause in 1879, in a land foreign to her. The grave of Begum Hazrat Mahal is in Kathmandu. On 10 May 1984, a Postage Stamp was issued in her honour. The indomitable Begum became one of the few women to fight against the British in the first war of Independence.

21. Bhimrao Ramji Ambedkar

Ambedkar in the 1950s

1st Minister of Law and Justice

In office

15 August 1947 – 6 October 1951

Prime Minister : Jawaharlal Nehru

Preceded by : Position established

Succeeded by : Charu Chandra Biswas

Member of Parliament, Rajya Sabha

from Bombay State

In office

3 April 1952 – 6 December 1956

Chairman of the Constitution Drafting

Committee

In office

29 August 1947 – 24 January 1950

Member of the Constituent Assembly of India

In office

9 December 1946 – 24 January 1950

Constituency • Bengal Province (1946–47)

• Bombay Province (1947–50)

Minister of Labour in Viceroy's Executive
Council

In office

22 July 1942 – 20 October 1946

Governors : The Marquess of Linlithgow

General : The Viscount Wavell

Preceded by : Feroz Khan Noon

Legislative positions

Personal details

Born :	Bhiva Ramji Sakpal
	14 April 1891
	Mhow, Central India Agency, British India (now Madhya Pradesh, India)
Died :	6 December 1956 (aged 65)
	New Delhi, India
Resting place :	Chaitya Bhoomi
	19°01'30"N 72°50'02"E
Political party :	Independent Labour Party
	Scheduled Castes Federation
Other political affiliations :	Republican Party of India
Spouses :	Ramabai Ambedkar (m. 1906; died 1935)
	Savita Ambedkar (m. 1948)

Children :   Yashwant

Relatives :   Ambedkar family

Education :   University of Mumbai (BA, MA)
                 Columbia University (MA, PhD)
                 London School of Economics (MSc,
                 DSc)

Profession :   Juristeconomistpoliticiansocial
                 reformerwriter

Awards :   Bharat Ratna (1990, posthumous)

Signature :

Nickname :   Babasaheb

Bhimrao Ramji Ambedkar (14 April 1891 – 6 December 1956), popularly known as Dr. Babasaheb Ambedkar was an Indian jurist, economist, politician, writer and social reformer. Bhimrao Ramji Ambedkar was an Indian jurist, economist, social reformer and political leader who headed the committee drafting the Constitution of India from the Constituent Assembly debates, served as Law and Justice minister in the first cabinet of Jawaharlal.

Babasaheb Ambedkar was a Freedom Fighter in True Sense. He fought for the Freedom of : Dalits and Harijans for their equal rights and their basic necessities. For their rights to Education. Bhimrao Ramji Ambedkar popularly known as Babasaheb, was an Indian jurist, economist, politician and social reformer who Chaired the Drafting Committee of the Constituent Assembly and was India's First Minister for Law and Justice.

He just used to sleep 3 hours in a day . He used to go to bed at 2 AM and would wake up at 5 . The whole time he would be reading or attending meetings . He never cared about any other thing except freedom for his people and thus wanted a way to free them and education was the only way for that. Ambedkar received his Ph.D. degree in economics at Columbia in 1927. In October 1916, he enrolled for the Bar course at Gray's Inn, and at the same time enrolled at the London School of Economics where he started working on a doctoral thesis. An economist and a reformer, Ambedkar played a pivotal role in shaping the Indian Constitution and served as the first Law Minister of Independent India. This year marks his 134th birthday and is being celebrated with enthusiasm nationwide. B.R Ambedkar's leadership as a social reformer remains unparalleled in modern Indian history. Faced with the entrenched caste system and institutionalised discrimination, Dr. Ambedkar spearheaded movements for the emancipation of the oppressed castes and untouchables.

22. Bipin Chandra Pal

Bipin Chandra Pal was an Indian nationalist, writer, orator, social reformer and freedom fighter. He was one third of the "Lal Bal Pal" triumvirate. He was one of the main architects of the Swadeshi movement. He is known as the Father of Revolutionary Thoughts in India.

Born: 7 November 1858, Habiganj Sadar Upazila, Bangladesh

Died: 20 May 1932 (age 73 years), Kolkata

Parents: Ramchandra Pal, Narayani Devi

Spouse: Birajmohini Devi (m. 1891), Nrityakali Devi (m. 1881)

Children: Niranjan Pal, Colin Pal

Education: University of Calcutta, Presidency University, St. Paul's Cathedral Mission College

Nick Name : Bengal Tiger

Bipin Chandra vociferously asserted the rights of the Indians in the third session of the Congress at Madras in 1887 by seconding the resolution for the repeal of the Arms Act, 1887. He criticized the Act for its undemocratic and discriminatory provisions regarding possession and carrying of arms by the Indians.

The famous quote of Bipin Chandra Pal:
"Freedom is no doubt a precious jewel, but it will remain such only as long as we are ready and willing to pay the price it demands." "When we stand, the Azad Hind Fauz has to be like a wall of granite; when we march, the Azad Hind Fauz has to be like a steamroller."

Bipin Chandra Pal leaves Congress because he had no faith in mild protests in the form of non-cooperation with the British colonial government. On that one issue, the assertive nationalist leader had nothing in common with Mahatma Gandhi. During the last six years of his life, he parted company with the Congress and led a secluded life. Bipin Chandra Pal started New India (Weekly) and Annie Besant started New India (Daily) to spread patriotic feelings in the people of India.

23. Chittaranjan Das

Chittaranjan Das, popularly called Deshbandhu, was an Indian freedom fighter, political activist and lawyer during the Indian Independence Movement and the Political Guru of Indian freedom fighter Netaji Subhas Chandra Bose.

Born: 5 November 1870, Tongibari, Bangladesh

Died: 16 June 1925 (age 54 years), Darjeeling

Party: Swaraj Party

Spouse: Basanti Devi (m. 1896–1925)

Children: Chiraranjan Das, Kalyani Debi, Aparna Debi

Organization founded: Swaraj Party

INDIA 1965 CHITTARANJAN DAS FIRST DAY COVER WITH SLOGAN '" MOVE WITH THE TIME USE AIRMAILS " CALCUTTA R.M.S.

Chittaranjan Das was born in Calcutta on 5 November 1870. His family were members of Brahmo Samaj. Das was the son of Bhuban Mohan Das, and nephew of the Brahmo social reformer Durga Mohan Das. His father was a solicitor and a journalist. In 1890, he graduated from the Presidency College. Within a few months of his graduation, he was sent by his father to England to compete for the Indian Civil Service. Chittaranjan Das, however, turned his attention to the study of Law and joined the Middle Temple. He was called to the English Bar in 1893. He is the founder-leader of the Swaraj Party in undivided Bengal during the period of British Colonial rule in India. His name is abbreviated as C. R. Das. Gandhiji was a great admirer of Das, and he called him a great spirit. The citizens gave him the honorary title 'Deshbandhu. Chittaranjan is well known for Chittaranjan Locomotive Works (CLW), which manufactures mainline diesel broad gauge locomotives. This factory commenced production in 1950; and up to 1972, it was involved in the production of broad gauge and meter gauge steam locomotives. He was highly influenced by Vivekananda's teachings and considered him as his spiritual Guru. Chittaranjan Das was the "Political Guru of Subhash Chandra Bose".

24. Dadabhai Naoroji

Dadabhai Naoroji, also known as the "Grand Old Man of India" and "Unofficial Ambassador of India", was an Indian Independence activist, political leader, merchant, scholar and writer who served as 2nd, 9th, and 22nd President of the Indian National Congress from 1886 to 1887, 1893 to 1894 and 1906 to 1907.

Born: 4 September 1825, Navsari

Died: 30 June 1917 (age 91 years), Mumbai

Organizations founded: East India Association

Children: Maki Dadina, Shirin Dadina

Education: Elphinstone College, University of Mumbai

Parents: Manekbai Naoroji Dordi, Naoroji Palanji Dordi

Dadabhai Naoroji is also known as the 'Grand Old Man of India' and worked as an Ambassador of India. He was a great politician, Indian scholar, and trader. Dadabhai Naoroji was the first Indian-Asian to be a British Member of Parliament. Naoroji was also one of the founding partners of the Indian National Congress. Dadabhai Naoroji was a renowned Indian freedom fighter and economic scholar. He played a pivotal role in the country's independence movement. Dadabhai Naoroji is often called the "Father of Indian Economics." His contributions to the field of economics are still studied and celebrated today. Dadabhai Naoroji was called Grand Old man of India due to his activities in Indian national movement for 6 decades. The East India Association was founded by Dadabhai Naoroji in 1866, in collaboration with Indians and retired British officials in London. In 1867, Dadabhai Naoroji proposed what is known as the 'economic imperialism' theory, in which he stated that British economic policies were completely draining India. He mentioned this theory in his book, Poverty and Un-British Rule in India, and it is also known as the 'Drain Theory'.

25. Gopal Krishna Gokhale

Gopal Krishna Gokhale CIE was an Indian political leader and a social reformer during the Indian independence movement, and political mentor of Indian freedom fighter Mahatma Gandhi. Gokhale was a senior leader of the Indian National Congress and the founder of the Servants of India Society.

Born: 9 May 1866, Kotluk
Died: 19 February 1915 (age 48 years), Mumbai
Organizations founded: Servants of India Society
Children: Kashibai, Godubai
Education: Elphinstone College (1884), Rajaram College
Parents: Krishna Rao Gokhale, Valubai Gokhale

Gopal Krishna Gokhale hailed from a Marathi Hindu Brahmin family of Ratnagiri, Bombay Presidency, now Maharashtra. He was born in a Chitpavan Brahmin family on 9 May 1866 of the British Raj in Kotluk village of Guhagar taluka in Ratnagiri district, in present-day Maharashtra (then part of the Bombay Presidency). Apart from being a senior leader of the Indian National Congress, he was the founder of the Servants of India Society. Through the Society as well as the Congress and other legislative bodies he served in, Gokhale campaigned for Indian self-rule and for social reforms. Bal Gangadhar tilak gave the title to Gopal Krishna Gokhale as "The Diamon of India". G.K.Gokhale: Gokhale was a senior leader of the Indian National Congress and also the founder of the Servants of India Society. Gandhi was deeply influenced by Gopal Krishna Gokhale and referred to him as his political guru. Gokhale encouraged Gandhi to tour India in a third-class railway compartment to understand India. He saw the nation with a very different point of view during his journey. He established the Servants of India Society and edited "Sudharak", a quarterly Journal of the Poona Sarvajanik Sabha. He was also appointed as a Companion of the Order of the Indian empire. Hitavada newspaper was started by him in 1911.

26. Kunwar Singh

Kunwar Singh, also known as Babu Kunwar Singh was a chief organiser of the Indian Rebellion of 1857 from the Bhojpur region of Bihar. He was originally the ruler of Jagdishpur estate. He led a selected band of armed soldiers against the troops under the command of the British East India Company.

Born : 13 November 1777, Jagdishpur

Died : 26 April 1858 (age 80 years), Jagdishpur

Parents : Raja Shahabzada Singh, Rani Panchratan Devi

Dynasty: Ujjainiya

Successor : Babu Amar Singh

Kunwar Singh (1777 – 26 April 1858) was a notable leader during the Indian Rebellion of 1857. He belonged to a royal Ujjainiya (Panwar) Rajput house of Jagdispur, currently a part of Bhojpur district, Bihar, India. Singh led the Indian Rebellion of 1857 in Bihar. He was nearly eighty and in failing health when he was called upon to take up arms. Kunwar Singh was the chieftain (zamindar) of the royal Rajput house of Jagdishpur, near Arrah, currently a part of Bhojpur district, Bihar State. He was enthroned in 1826 following the death of his father Raja Sahabzada Singh. A British hunter who lived in India's Kaladhungi and Nainital was seen by Jim Corbett. Kunwar Singh, the leader of Chandni Chawk and an excellent hunter, was one of his closest friends. At the age of eight, Corbett's friend Kunwar was the first to congratulate him on getting his first firearm. In March 1858, Kunwar Singh occupied Azamgarh (now in UP). He later returned to his home and led a victorious battle near Jagdispur on 23rd July. The British led by Captain le Grand were defeated in this battle although Kunwar Singh was badly injured.

27. Sarojini Naidu

Sarojini Naidu was an Indian political activist and poet who served as the first Governor of United Provinces, after India's independence. She played an important role in the Indian independence movement against the British Raj.

Born: 13 February 1879, Hyderabad

Died: 2 March 1949 (age 70 years), Lucknow

Spouse: Muthyala Govindarajulu Naidu (m. 1898–1949)

Children: Padmaja Naidu, Jayasurya Naidu, Leelamani Naidu, Randheer Naidu, Nilawar Naidu

Parents: Aghorenath Chattopadhyay, Barada Sundari Devi

Education: King's College London (1895–1898), Nizam College

Sarojini Naidu (born February 13, 1879, Hyderabad, India—died March 2, 1949,

Lucknow) was a political activist, feminist, poet, and the first Indian woman to be president of the Indian National Congress and to be appointed an Indian state governor. She was an exceptional student with knowledge of Urdu, Telegu, English, Bengali and Persian. Her remarkable passion for writing from an early age earned her a scholarship to study abroad. She was sometimes called "the Nightingale of India." Her work as a poet earned her the sobriquet 'the Nightingale of India', or 'Bharat Kokila' by Mahatma Gandhi because of color, imagery and lyrical quality of her poetry. Naidu's poetry includes both children's poems and others written on more serious themes including patriotism, romance, and tragedy. Sarojini Naidu was elected as the President of the Indian National Congress Party in 1925, the first ever woman to assume that position. In an expression of hope and courage, she said, " In the battle for liberty, fear is one unforgivable treachery and despair, the one unforgivable sin". Participation in Quit India Movement: Sarojini Naidu registered her participation in Quit India Movement launched in 1942 as well. Advocacy for Women's Rights: Naidu is known for championing the cause of women's rights in India.

28. K. M. Munshi

Kanhaiyalal Maneklal Munshi, popularly known by his pen name Ghanshyam Vyas, was an Indian independence movement activist, politician, writer from Gujarat state. A lawyer by profession, he later turned to author and politician. He is a well-known name in Gujarati literature.

Born: 30 December 1887, Bharuch

Died: 8 February 1971 (age 83 years), Mumbai

Previous offices: Governor of Uttar Pradesh (1952–1957)

Organizations founded: Bharatiya Vidya Bhavan's College

Education: The Maharaja Sayajirao University of Baroda

Full name: Kanaiyalal Maneklal Munshi

Born on December 30, 1887, and passing away on February 8, 1971, Kanhaiyalal Maneklal Munshi was a Gujarati politician, writer, and educator who was active in the Indian independence struggle. He was also known by his pen name, Ghanshyam Vyas. Munshi was on the ad hoc Flag Committee that selected the Flag of India in August 1947, and on the committee which drafted the Constitution of India under the chairmanship of B. R. Ambedkar. Besides being a politician and educator, Munshi was also an environmentalist. Works of K. M. Munshi. Munshi's literary works are celebrated for their depth and insight. His novels like Patan-ni-Prabhuta (The Glory of Patan), Gujarat-no-Nath (The Lord and Master of Gujarat), and Rajadhiraj (The King of Kings) are some of the best-known historical books in Gujarati. Munshi had a vision of free India in terms, not only merely of political freedom, constitutional democracy and social diversity but in terms of its culture, tradition and the rich heritage of wisdom and learning. In order to foster ethical, moral, spiritual, intellectual and global values.

29. Tantia Tope

Tantia Tope was a notable commander in the Indian Rebellion of 1857.

Born: 16 February 1814, Yeola

Died: 18 April 1859 (age 45 years), Shivpuri

Full name: Ramachandra Pandurang Tope

Parents: Pandurang Rao Tope, Rukhmabai

Tantia Tope, also spelt Tatya Tope or Tantia Topi, was a leader of the Indian Mutiny of 1857–58. His real name was Ramchandra Panduranga. He was present at Nana Sahib's massacre of the British colony in Kanpur; in early November 1857 he had taken command of the rebel forces of the state of Gwalior and driven Gen. C.A. Windham into his entrenchments at Kanpur on November 27–28.

1) Tatya Tope was one of the freedom fighters who fought against the Britishers.

2) Tatya Tope was also one of the main revolutionaries in the revolt of 1857.

3) Tatya Tope was born in 1814 at Yeola in the Nashik district of Maharashtra.

4) Tatya Tope was very close to Nana Sahib, the adopted son of Peshwa Bajirao II.

5) In the revolt of 1857, Tatya Tope was the closest military aide of Nana Sahib.

6) Tatya Tope was one of the leaders in the massacre of Cawnpore (Kanpur) in 1857.

7) By November 1857 Tatya Tope took forces to recapture Gwalior to capture Kanpur.

8) Tatya Tope along with Nana Sahib helped Rani Lakshmi Bai to protect Jhansi.

9) In order to capture Kanpur Tatya Tope was defeated by the British forces in 1859.

10) After getting caught by British forces, Tatya Tope was executed on 18th April 1859.

30. C. Rajagopalachari

Chakravarti Rajagopalachari BR, popularly known as Rajaji or C.R., also known as Mootharignar Rajaji, was an Indian statesman, writer, lawyer, and Indian independence activist. Rajagopalachari was the last Governor-General of India, as when India became a republic in 1950 the office was abolished.

Born: 10 December 1878, Thorapalli Agraharam

Died: 25 December 1972 (age 94 years), Chennai

Previous offices: Chief Minister of Tamil Nadu (1952–1954)

Party: Indian National Congress

Awards: Bharat Ratna

Full name: Chakravarti Rajagopalachari

Chakravarti Rajagopalachari (10 December 1878 – 25 December 1972), informally called Rajaji or C.R., was an Indian lawyer, Indian independence activist, politician, writer, politician and leader of the Indian National Congress who served as the last Governor-General of India. Rajagopalachari founded the Swatantra Party and was one of the first recipients of India's highest civilian award, the Bharat Ratna. He vehemently opposed the use of nuclear weapons and was a proponent of world peace and disarmament. During his lifetime, he also acquired the nickname 'Mango of Salem'. C. Rajagopalachari's formula (or C. R. formula or Rajaji formula) was a proposal formulated by Chakravarti Rajagopalachari to solve the political deadlock between the All India Muslim League and the Indian National Congress on the independence of British India. Upon independence in August 1947, the title of Viceroy was abolished. The representative of the British Sovereign became known once again as the Governor-General. C. Rajagopalachari became the only Indian Governor-General. He had been the last Governor-General of India and one of the first recipients of India's highest civilian award, the Bharat Ratna.

31. Abdul Hafiz Mohamed Barakatullah

Abdul Hafiz Mohamed Barakatullah, known with his honorific as Maulana Barakatullah (c. 7 July 1854 – 20 September 1927) was an anti-British Indian revolutionary with sympathy for the Pan-Islamic movement. Barakatullah was born on 7 July 1854 at Itwra Mohalla Bhopal in Madhya Pradesh, India.

Born: 7 July 1854, Bhopal

Died: 20 September 1927 (age 73 years), San Francisco, California, United States

Barakatullah was born on 7 July 1854 at Itawra mohalla, Bhopal in what is today Madhya Pradesh, India. He fought from outside India, with fiery speeches and revolutionary writings in leading newspapers, for the independence of India. He did not live to see India's independence. In 1915, Maulana Barakatullah Bhopali reached Kabul to participate in the ongoing Ghadar wave against the British from America to Afghanistan. He participated in this movement and made further strategies for the campaign to liberate India. Barakatullah University formerly known as Bhopal University was established in 1970 in the capital city of Madhya Pradesh. In 1988 it was rechristened as Barakatullah Vishwavidyalaya, In the living memory of the great freedom fighter Prof. Barakatullah who belonged to Bhopal.

32. Maulana Hasrat Mohani

Maulana Hasrat Mohani was born on 1 January 1875 in Qasba Mohan of Unnao district in Uttar Pradesh. The real name of Maulana Hasrat Mohani was Syed Fazal-ul-Hasan. Hasrat was his takhallus (a nickname used for poetry or ghazals) that he also used while he penned down poetry.

Born: 1 January 1875, Mohan
Died: 13 May 1951 (age 76 years), Lucknow
Party: Communist Party of India
Full name: Syed Fazlul Hasan Hasrat Mohani
Education: MAO College, Aligarh Muslim University
Books: Hasarata Mohānī
Known for: Famous Slogan Inquilab Zindabad

Syed Fazl-ul-Hasan (1 January 1875 – 13 May 1951), known by his pen-name Hasrat Mohani, was an Indian activist, freedom fighter in the Indian independence movement and a noted poet of the Urdu language. He coined the notable slogan Inquilab Zindabad (translation of "Long live the revolution!") in 1921. According to a few historians, Maulana Hasrat Mohani wrote the slogan 'Inquilab Zindabad' in 1921. This is the same slogan that Bhagat Singh immortalized forever in the memory of the nation. Inquilab Zindabad, can be translated as "Long Live Revolution". was coined by Moulana Hasrat Mohani in the year 1921. It was one of the most famous slogans during the Indian freedom struggle. It was used by Shahid-e-Azam Bhagat Singh through his speeches and writings in the early 1920s. Maulana Hasrat Mohani was the first congress activist to demand complete independence (Poorna Swaraj) from the British in the Ahmedabad session of congress in 1921. Mohani actively participated in the freedom struggle and was imprisoned on several occasions. He also played an important role in the Khilafat movement. In 1921, Mohani along with Swami Kumaranand moved a resolution at the annual session of the Congress Party, where he called for complete independence.

33. Yusuf Meherally

Yusuf Meherally was an Indian freedom fighter and socialist leader. He was elected the Mayor of Bombay in 1942 while he was imprisoned in the Yerawada Central Prison. The son of a well-to-do businessman, Yusuf Meherally was born in Bombay on 3 September 1903.

Born: 23 September 1903, Mumbai

Died: 1950 (age 47 years)

Previous office: Mayor of Bombay (1942–1943)

Movement: Quit India Movement; Indian independence movement

The iconic 'Quit India' slogan was coined by socialist Congress leader and lesser-known hero of the Indian National movement Yusuf Meher Ali in 1942. He was the founder of National Militia, Bombay youth League, and the Congress Socialist Party. The slogan "Simon Go Back", which was coined by Yusuf Meherally upon the Commission's arrival in Bombay, echoed throughout their journey in various parts of the Subcontinent. He was a part of the Quit India Movement along with Mahatma Gandhi for India's last nationwide campaign for independence from the British Empire. He was a participant of underground movement and was in forefront of Quit India Movement. Yusuf Meherally was an Indian freedom fighter and socialist leader. He was elected the Mayor of Bombay in 1942 while he was imprisoned in the Yerawada Central Prison.

34. Bankin Chandra Chatterji

Bankim Chandra Chattopadhyay CIE was an Indian novelist, poet, essayist and journalist. He was the author of the 1882 Bengali language novel Anandamath, which is one of the landmarks of modern Bengali and Indian literature.

Born: 26 June 1838, British Raj

Died: 8 April 1894 (age 55 years), Kolkata

Spouse: Mohini Devi (m. 1849–1859)

Education: Presidency College (1856–1857), University of Calcutta, Hooghly Mohsin College, Hooghly Collegiate School

Siblings: Sanjeeb Chandra Chattopadhyay

Parents: Yadav Chandra Chattopadhyaya, Durgadebi Chattopadhyaya

Bankim Chandra Chatterjee: He was an Indian poet and journalist. He composed the national song Vande Mataram, the national song of India during India's freedom struggle. One of the most influential literary figures of the 19th century was Bankim Chandra Chatterjee, also known as Bankim Chandra Chattopadhyay. He was born on 27 June 1838, in Naihati, Bengal Presidency, British India, which is now part of West Bengal, India. Bankim Chandra Chatterjee wrote the national song Vande Mataram. It is a poem written in Sanskrit by Bankim Chandra Chatterjee in his Bengali novel Anandamath. It later was made the National Song of our country. Vande Mataram was first sung by Rabindranath Tagore in 1896. It was adopted by the constituent assembly on 24th January 1950. The music is composed by Jadhunath Bhattacharya.

35. Muhammad Iqbal

Sir Muhammad Iqbal was a South Asian Islamic philosopher, poet and politician. His poetry is considered to be among the greatest of the 20th century, and his vision of a cultural and political ideal for the Muslims of British-ruled India is widely regarded as having animated the impulse for the Pakistan Movement.

Born: 9 November 1877, Sialkot, Pakistan

Died: 21 April 1938 (age 60 years), Lahore, Pakistan

Influenced by: Rumi, Friedrich Nietzsche, Bulleh Shah

Children: Javed Iqbal, Aftab Iqbal, Muneera Bano, Miraj Begum

Spouse: Sardar Begum

Iqbal was born on 9 November 1877 in a Punjabi-Kashmiri family from Sialkot in the Punjab Province of British India (now in Pakistan). His family traced their ancestry back to the Sapru clan of Kashmiri Pandits who were from a south Kashmiri village in Kulgam and converted to Islam in the 15th century. Muhammad Iqbal (born November 9, 1877, Sialkot, Punjab, India [now in Pakistan]—died April 21, 1938, Lahore, Punjab) was a poet and philosopher known for his influential efforts to direct his fellow Muslims in British-administered India toward the establishment of a separate Muslim state, an aspiration that was eventually realized in the country of Pakistan. He was knighted in 1922. Muhammad Iqbal, also known as Allama Iqbal, is the National Poet of Pakistan. A poet, philosopher, politician, lawyer, and scholar, Iqbal was born on November 9, 1877, in Punjab, Pakistan, to Kashmiri parents and educated at Scotch Mission College in Sialkot.